FOR
SANIBEL

The Delaplaine
2021 Long Weekend Guide

Andrew Delaplaine

**NO BUSINESS HAS PAID A SINGLE PENNY OR GIVEN _ANYTHING_
TO BE INCLUDED IN THIS BOOK.**

Senior Editors - *Renee & Sophie Delaplaine*
Senior Writer - **James Cubby**

Gramercy Park Press
New York London Paris

Please submit corrections, additions or comments to
<u>andrewdelaplaine@mac.com</u>

FORT MYERS & SANIBEL
The Delaplaine
Long Weekend Guide

TABLES OF CONTENTS

WHY FORT MYERS & SANIBEL?

Ah, the tranquility of Fort Myers (and by Fort Myers, we mean Fort Myers Beach, Sanibel, Captiva, the whole area).

In the "historic" downtown district, you'll see some interesting architecture from the Victorian period as well as the early 20th Century. There are numerous cafes, courtyards, little shops.

The simple truth about Fort Myers is that if Thomas Edison hadn't decided to move here in 1885 to mend his health after his first wife died, this place probably wouldn't be much different from any of the hundreds of little no-name towns dotting both Florida coasts. Fort Myers is about the same distance from Tampa as it is from Miami (150 miles), something people find hard to believe, since it's on the "west coast."

There's not much else to see in Fort Myers besides Edison's house (as well as that of his neighbor and friend, Henry Ford). After that, head to the causeway for the 15-mile drive (starting southwest on McGregor Boulevard for 10 miles, then turning left onto San Carlos Boulevard) to Fort Myers Beach. This takes about a half hour if there's not heavy traffic.

SANIBEL ISLAND
A popular family-friendly vacation spot where you can find lots to keep the kids occupied. Lots of white

sand, beach activities, shopping, golf, restaurants, and family accommodations. Many hotels offer kid's programs. The island boasts lush tropical foliage and crystal blue water. It's only a 3-mile causeway ride away from the comparatively busy Fort Myers.

Some 70% of the island is preserved as wildlife refuge, which is good for us and good for the wildlife. Here you won't see stoplights, billboards, or even street lamps. No high-rise buildings either.

The Calusa Indians lived here for some 5,000 years until invading Europeans wiped them out. (I wonder what the Calusa policy was toward illegal immigrants. LOL.)

These Indians used the plentiful shells that washed up on the pristine beaches (that much hasn't changed—the beaches are prehistorically perfect) for everything from weapons to money to bodily decorations like necklaces. Because Sanibel and its western neighbor Captiva are situated east-west rather than north-south, they catch shells churned up by the Gulf currents.

One of the world's largest mangrove stands is here, and you can see for yourself the manatees, alligators, conchs and other creatures that come here for shelter.

The locals are quick to point out the difference between a "refuse" and a "park." Parks are for people, they'll tell you, and refuges are for animals.

President Truman established this refuge in 1945, convinced by political cartoonist J.N. "Ding" Darling.

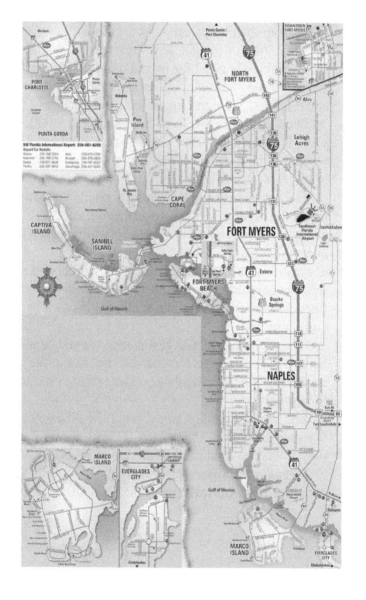

GETTING AROUND

You'll need a car. It's hard to do anything without one. You might as well pick it up at the Southwest Florida International Airport, which serves the area. (It's about 20 minutes from downtown Fort Myers.)

If you take a taxi into town, it'll run about $35, higher for Fort Myers Beach and Sanibel and Captiva islands. (Cheaper to rent the car.)

The nearest **Amtrak** station is in Tampa (800-872-7245; www.amtrak.com). They have bus service to Fort Myers, using the Greyhound station at 2275 Cleveland Avenue. (**Greyhound**, 800-231-2222; www.greyhound.com).

WHERE TO STAY

CASA YBEL RESORT
2255 W Gulf Dr, Sanibel, 239-472-3145
www.casaybelresort.com
This is one of the only all-suite beachfront resorts in
Sanibel Island. The resort is decorated to feel like
home, but of course it doesn't really. What it does
offer is beautiful views of the Gulf of Mexico that
you probably don't have at home. Amenities include:
free Wi-Fi, outdoor gas grills, fully equipped
kitchens, premium linens, screened-in patios and free
copies of the New York Times & Wall Street Journal.
Kids Club & Family programs available.

CASTAWAYS BEACH & BAY COTTAGES

6460 Sanibel Captiva Rd, Sanibel, 239-472-1252
www.castawayssanibel.com/
A rustic property of standalone cottages with 40
rooms is set on a narrow strip of land between Sanibel
and Captiva islands. Amenities include:
Complimentary Wi-Fi, free parking, outdoor pool,
beach umbrellas, and barbecue grills. Pet friendly.
Boat tours, kayaking, rowing, canoeing, and biking
rentals available.

DIAMONDHEAD BEACH RESORT

2000 Estero Blvd., Fort Myers Beach, 855-516-6650
www.diamondheadfl.com
Here in this 12-story oceanfront resort property you
can expect to find larger than average 1-bedroom.
One of the big treats here are the sliding glass doors
that give onto the capacious balconies (each room has

a private 700-sq.-ft. balcony). Try to get a flat on a higher floor. The views are substantially better. Another plus: the couch in the living room folds out into a bed. $$$

EDGEWATER INN
781 Estero Blvd., Fort Myers Beach, 239-463-0700
www.edgewaterinnfmb.com
Not on the beach, but only 200 or 300 feet from it is this quiet little inn. Has two 1-bedroom suites and four 2-bedroom suites. Screened in porches are nice. In the winter season, you have to book by the week. In the summer, they need a 3-day minimum, perfect for your Long Weekend visit. A BBQ outside is available for your use, as well as beach chairs and bikes and that like. (Closed from July-Sept.)
$$

EMBASSY SUITES FORT MYERS-ESTERO
10450 Corkscrew Commons Dr. (Off of I-75 and
Corkscrew Rd.), Estero, 239-949-4222
embassysuites3.hilton.com/
Nestled against the 16-acre Estero Bay Preserve State
Park and near the beach is this
all-suite full-service hotel close to Miromar Outlets,
Gulf Coast Town Center, Germaine Arena and
Florida Gulf Coast University. Free airport shuttle,
which you can also use to visit spots within a 5-mile
radius of the hotel. On site Hertz desk. Choose from
150 two-room suites which include free WiFi, views
of the garden atrium or the outdoor swimming pool.
Expect a wet bar, coffeemaker, microwave and
refrigerator in each suite.
Free cooked-to-order breakfast. On site **Eagle's Nest
Café and Lounge**. Also a fitness center.

FAIRFIELD INN BY MARRIOTT

7090 Cypress Terrace, Fort Myers, 239-437-5600
www.marriott.com
Conveniently located; 3 floors with 104 rooms. Free
breakfast includes hot waffles, Jimmy Dean Breakfast
sandwich & fresh fruit. Heated outdoor pool & hot
tub, exercise room, and guest laundry. Free parking.
Free high-speed Internet. This is a smoke-free hotel.
$$

HIBISCUS HOUSE BED & BREAKFAST

2135 McGregor Blvd., Fort Myers, 239-332-2651
www.thehibiscushouse.net
Built in 1922, Hibiscus House has been lovingly
restored. The guest rooms (private baths) are
individually furnished, each with French doors
opening onto a private terrace. Free WiFi. Pet friendly
rooms available. $$-$$$

ISLAND INN

3111 W Gulf Dr, Sanibel, 239-472-1561
www.islandinnsanibel.com
This friendly inn, dating from 1895 but recently refurbished, is located on 10 acres, and offers a variety of hotel suites – many with beautiful Gulf views. Though it has a lot of "Old Florida" touches, like tables inlaid with some of the shells that are so famously gathered on the beaches here, and screened in porches that remind us that there once was a time when there was no a/c, it has lots of modern amenities like daily maid service, free Wi-Fi, flatscreen HD TVs, cable TV, iPod/iPhone docking stations, use of private beach, free beach chairs, tennis courts, shuffleboard, horseshoes, heated pool and sundeck. On-site restaurant.

SANIBEL HARBOUR RESORT & SPA

17260 Harbour Pointe Dr., Fort Myers, 239-466-4000
www.marriott.com/hotels/travel/rswsb-sanibel-harbour-marriott-resort-and-spa/

Hard to beat the location of this 300+ room resort: it's an 80+ acre parcel on a point overlooking San Carlos Bay and Sanibel and Captiva islands. From this

vantage point, each room (they all have balconies) has splendid views. They sport 3 pools and a beach on the bay, a big fitness center & health club, kids' programs, clay tennis courts, classes, clinic, etc. The Spa here has dozens of treatments, highlighted by the BETAR bed, one of only a few in the world. (This contraption smothers the body in sound waves which apparently induces a state of tranquil meditation. I obviously haven't tried it myself.)

With the half-dozen restaurants and a lounge they have, you could easily check in here and not leave and have a pretty good time of it. $$$$

SEASIDE INN
541 E Gulf Dr, Sanibel, 239-472-1400
www.theinnsofsanibel.com/sanibel-inn
This inn offers an ideal island getaway with 91 guest rooms, suites and two-bedroom condos featuring beautiful views of the Gulf of Mexico. Amenities

include: heated outdoor swimming pool, on-site Sea Star Café, poolside tiki bar, and live entertainment.

SUPER 8
2717 Colonial Blvd., Fort Myers, 239-240-8726
www.super8.com
Conveniently located near downtown with easy access to local attractions. Outdoor pool. Free parking and free Wi-Fi. $

TWEEN WATERS
15951 Captiva Drive, Captiva Island, 239-472-5161
www.tween-waters.com
This small resort offers 137 smoke-free rooms equipped with small fridges. The resort features a marina, an outdoor pool and full-service spa. Private beach. Amenities include: Complimentary buffet

breakfast, complimentary Wi-Fi, in-room safes, video games and cable TV. Outdoor activities available include kayak and bike rentals. On-site restaurant, **Old Captiva House**, features fresh seafood. Cocktails are available at the **Crow's Nest**. Nearby activities available include fishing, boating, tennis and golf.

WHERE TO EAT

Ridiculously Expensive
Sensible Alternatives
Quality Bargain Options

BAHAMA BREEZE
14701 S Tamiami Trl, Fort Myers, 239-454-9234
www.bahamabreeze.com
CUISINE: Seafood/Latin American
DRINKS: Full Bar

SERVING: Lunch & Dinner
PRICE RANGE: $$
Casual chain eatery serving a variety of Caribbean and Mexican inspired dishes. Favorites: Beef & Chicken empanadas and Trinidad chicken curry bowl. Half-price appetizers served before 6 p.m. Happy Hour specials. Popular with families.

BEACH PIERSIDE GRILL AND BLOWFISH BAR

1000 Estero Blvd., Fort Myers Beach, 239-765-7800
www.piersidegrill.com
CUISINE: American
DRINKS: Full bar
SERVING: Lunch & Dinner
PRICE RANGE: $$
Located on the beach next to the public pier. Open for lunch and dinner. Great food and atmosphere.
Blowfish bar is always busy and serves their famous frozen cocktails.

BLEU RENDEZ-VOUS FRENCH BISTRO

2430 Periwinkle Way, Near Tarpon Bay
Road, Sanibel Island, 239-565-1608
www.bleurendezvous.com
CUISINE: French/Seafood
DRINKS: Beer & Wine Only
SERVING: Dinner; closed Sunday & Monday
PRICE RANGE: $$$
Old-world style eatery offering refined French dishes.
Favorites: Yellowtail snapper and Surf & Turf (petit
filet mignon, 2 lamb chops and a 4 – ounce prawn).
Nice wine selection. Outdoor seating available. Try
the crème brûlée – it's divine.

BONGO'S BEACH BAR AND GRILL
PINK SHELL RESORT

275 Estero Blvd, Fort Myers Beach, 239-463-8614

www.pinkshell.com/restaurants-dining/bongos-beach-bar/

CUISINE: American Traditional
DRINKS: Full Bar
SERVING: Lunch, Dinner
PRICE RANGE: $$
NEIGHBORHOOD: Fort Myers Beach
Beachfront dining with a tropical flair. Nothing quaint. It's a big modern beach resort with tons of outdoor dining under umbrellas overlooking the pool and beach. Has one of those "something for everyone" menus, with flatbreads, burgers, frozen drinks, sandwiches, salads, pizzas, quesadillas, tacos, chicken wings. Favorites: Pink Gulf Shrimp and Florida Black Grouper. Great tropical cocktails. Beautiful sunsets over the water, so this is a naturally attractive happy hour destination.

CABAÑAS BEACH BAR & GRILL
DiamondHead Beach Resort
2000 Estero Blvd., Fort Myers Beach, 239-765-7654

www.chloesfl.com/cabanas-beach-bar
CUISINE: American (new)
DRINKS: Full bar
SERVING: Lunch & Dinner
PRICE RANGE: $$
Beach Bar & Grill serving salads, sandwiches, and wraps. Bar serves tropical cocktails. Live entertainment every Saturday (1 – 4 p.m.)

CAPE COD FISH COMPANY
15501 Old McGregor Blvd, Fort Myers, 239-313-6462
www.capecodfishco.com
CUISINE: Seafood
DRINKS: Full Bar
SERVING: Lunch & Dinner; Closed Mondays
PRICE RANGE: $$
NEIGHBORHOOD: Fort Myers
With corrugated metal sheets as a prime interior design motif, and somewhat "nautical" décor elements, this storefront in a strip mall does its best to impart a New England "Seafood Shack" feel. This extends to the seafood-focused menu where they offer New England style dishes (as opposed to the usual Florida-Caribbean slant one usually gets in these parts), like a steamer of Ipswich Clams; Whole belly fried clams and other baskets; Lobster rolls; several chowders (the Lobster & Corn is really tasty, thick and bursting with flavors). There's a Fried seafood platter and Blackened salmon tacos, but what I really liked was the Scallops Rockefeller. Hadn't had that before.

CHLOË'S RESTAURANT & LOUNGE
DiamondHead Beach Resort
2000 Estero Blvd., Fort Myers Beach, 239-765-0595
www.chloesfl.com/chloes-lounge
CUISINE: American
DRINKS: Full bar
SERVING: Lunch & Dinner
PRICE RANGE: $$$
Casual beachside dining with tropical cocktails. Live entertainment. Happy Hour 5 – 7 p.m.

CIBO
12901 McGregor Blvd, Ste 17, Fort Myers, 239-454-3700
www.cibofortmyers.com
CUISINE: Italian
DRINKS: Beer & Wine Only
SERVING: Dinner; closed Mondays
PRICE RANGE: $$$
Modern upscale eatery serving classic Italian dishes. Menu picks: Polpette Alla Casalinga (variety of meatballs in red sauce) and Chicken Marsala. Nice variety of wines. Happy hour specials.

THE CLAM SHACK
2407 Periwinkle Way, Sanibel Island, 239-472-6882
www.theclamshacksanibel.com
CUISINE: Seafood/Burgers
DRINKS: Beer & Wine
SERVING: Lunch & Dinner
PRICE RANGE: $$
Friendly family-style eatery serving fresh New England seafood flown in four times a week.

Favorites: Shrimp sandwich and Maine Lobster rolls. Fish and Chips are also worth mentioning. Popular lunch spot. Outdoor seating.

COCONUTS POOL BAR
CASA YBEL RESORT
2255 W Gulf Dr, Sanibel, 239-472-3145
www.casaybelresort.com/
CUISINE: Southern/Seafood
DRINKS: Full Bar
SERVING: Breakfast, Lunch
PRICE RANGE: $$$
NEIGHBORHOOD: Sanibel Island
Cute little bar located next to the pool, but it's NOT CHEAP. Favorites: Shrimp crab wrap and Grilled grouper sandwich. Creative cocktails.

CONNORS STEAK & SEAFOOD
10076 Gulf Center Dr, Fort Myers, 239-267-2677
www.connorsrestaurant.com

CUISINE: Steakhouse
DRINKS: Full Bar
SERVING: Lunch & Dinner
PRICE RANGE: $$$
Casual eatery serving fresh seafood, premium aged steaks, pastas, and salads. Favorites: Filet Mignon (of course) and Lobster/blue crab bisque. Great selection of wines.

DOC FORD'S RUM BAR & GRILLE

708 Fisherman's Wharf, Fort Myers Beach, 239-765-9660

5400 South Seas Plantation Rd, Captiva, 239-312-4275

2500 Island Inn Rd, Sanibel, 239-472-8311

www.docfords.com/

CUISINE: Seafood
DRINKS: Full Bar
SERVING: Lunch, Dinner
PRICE RANGE: $$
NEIGHBORHOOD: Fort Myers Beach, Sanibel Island and Captiva
Casual eatery with three locations locally, each with a little something different to offer. Waterfront dining. Favorites: Penne pasta with shrimp and Fish tacos. Tropical cocktails. Live music.

THE DOGHOUSE

1207 Estero Blvd, Fort Myers Beach, 239-940-1043
https://doghousefmb.com/
CUISINE: American
DRINKS: Full Bar
SERVING: Lunch, Dinner (10 to 8)

PRICE RANGE: $
NEIGHBORHOOD: Fort Myers Beach
Casual inexpensive eatery with an outdoor counter offering a menu of comfort-food basics like burgers, hot dogs, and cheesesteaks. They also have breakfast (The Sausage Skillet is great—Kielbasa, peppers, onions, mushrooms and home fries topped off with 2 eggs.) The key here is the really high-quality ingredients used in all these dishes which makes everything jump with flavor. (Try the Island Jerk Chicken sandwich if you don't believe me.) Kids' menu. Great place for a quick snack or a family-friendly breakfast, lunch or dinner.

GEORGE & WENDY'S SANIBEL SEAFOOD GRILLE
2499 Periwinkle Way, Sanibel Island, 239-395-1263
www.sanibelseafoodgrille.com

CUISINE: American/Seafood
DRINKS: Full Bar
SERVING: Lunch & Dinner
PRICE RANGE: $$
Popular casual eatery serving seafood and classic American dishes. Favorites: Shrimp Scampi and Cajun chicken pasta. Full bar with beer on tap. Outdoor seating and lots of TVs to watch sports. Excellent desserts. Open later than most places over here.

GRAMMA DOT'S SEASIDE SALOON
634 N Yachtsman Dr, Sanibel Island, 239-472-8138
www.sanibelmarina.com/gramma.html
CUISINE: Seafood
DRINKS: Beer & Wine Only
SERVING: Lunch & Dinner
PRICE RANGE: $$
The place with its white-painted cathedral ceilings and simple atmosphere is a popular seafood eatery. Has a roomy bar area as well as tables against the windows, which overlook a marina. There's also seating outside under a permanent awning, if you want to get even closer to the water. Favorites: Blackened grouper salad and Popcorn shrimp. Small variety of wines and beer – a couple of local beers on tap. Family friendly.

GREEN CUP CAFÉ
1412 Dean St, Fort Myers, 239-200-8679
https://www.facebook.com/organicgreencupcafe/
CUISINE: Smoothies/Raw Juices
DRINKS: No Booze
SERVING: Lunch & Dinner; closed Sun
PRICE RANGE: $$
A place for the healthy minded. Menu includes
organic raw juices, smoothies, teas, raw and vegan
desserts, salads, and wraps.

HAROLD'S
15250 S Tamiami Trl, Suite 107, Fort Myers, 239-
849-0622
www.haroldscuisine.com
CUISINE: American (New)
DRINKS: Beer & Wine Only

SERVING: Dinner; closed Sun, Mon & Tues
PRICE RANGE: $$$
Upscale eatery offering inventive menu of American
fare. Favorites: House-made buratta with ripe
tomatoes & pesto and Grilled octopus. Nice selection
of desserts and dessert wines, unusual for this area.

IL CIELO
1244 Periwinkle Way, Sanibel Island, 239-472-5555
www.ilcielosanibel.com
CUISINE: American (New)/Seafood/Mediterranean
DRINKS: Full Bar
SERVING: Dinner; closed Mondays
PRICE RANGE: $$$
Beautiful upscale restaurant with an impressive menu.
Favorites: Seared Day-Boat Scallops and Free-Range
Chicken Picatta. Nice bar and impressive wine list.
Key lime pie with raspberry drizzle is a must. Live
piano music.

THE ISLAND COW
2163 Periwinkle Way, Sanibel, 239-472-0606
www.sanibelislandcow.com/
CUISINE: Seafood/American (New)
DRINKS: Full Bar
SERVING: Breakfast, Lunch & Dinner
PRICE RANGE: $$
A casual family café offering a menu of American cuisine and raw-bar selections. Menu favorites include Burgers and Conch Fritters. Outdoor seating. Live music at night.

KJ'S FRESH GRILL
10950 S Cleveland Ave, Fort Myers, 239-275-4745
www.kjsfreshgrill.com
CUISINE: Seafood/Steakhouse
DRINKS: Full Bar
SERVING: Lunch & Dinner
PRICE RANGE: $$
Casual eatery offering a nice selection of seafood, steaks, and burgers. Favorites: Prime Rib and Fresh Gulf Cobia. Signature cocktails and craft beer.

LAZY FLAMINGO, BOKEELIA

16501 Stringfellow Rd, Bokeelia, 239-283-5959
https://www.facebook.com/pages/Lazy-Flamingo/163551320376209
CUISINE: Seafood
DRINKS: Full Bar
SERVING: Lunch & Dinner
PRICE RANGE: $$
This super casual fish shack is not easy to find, but you'll be glad once you do. Menu favorites include: Conch fritters, steamed shrimp, and Fried Grouper sandwich. But what you ought to get is their signature item, **The Pot** (two dozen oysters or clams steamed in

beer, their special spice mix, onions and celery. Get the Flamingo Garlic Bread to go with it. If you're still hungry, go for the conch chowder (some of the best I've ever had) or a very satisfying grouper sandwich.

LIGHTHOUSE CAFÉ
362 Periwinkle Way, Sanibel, 239-472-0303
www.lighthousecafe.com
CUISINE: Breakfast
DRINKS: Beer & Wine Only
SERVING: Brunch & Breakfast
PRICE RANGE: $$
A popular retro-style café (the walls are covered with prints of beacons and lighthouse themes) offering home-style cooking. Great place for breakfast (they claim to have the "World's Best Breakfast') with favorites like Eggs Benedict (served on a croissant and topped with Key Lime hollandaise no less) and their popular Belgian Waffles. The pancakes are made with waffle flour, which adds a different twist. Popular spot so there's often a wait for a table.

MAD HATTER RESTAURANT
6467 Sanibel Captiva Rd, Sanibel, 239-472-0033
www.madhatterrestaurant.com
CUISINE: Seafood
DRINKS: Beer & Wine Only
SERVING: Dinner; closed Mondays
PRICE RANGE: $$$
Upscale waterfront eatery that has white tablecloth service, but mixed with a charming "Alice in Wonderland" theme that carries through the whole place, with every wall surface covered with Alice

murals, Alice stained glass, and shelves stuffed with toys and other items evoking the classic fairy tale. There's a nice garden outside. Has a menu of New American cuisine and seafood. Menu picks: Phylo shrimp; Vegetable risotto that's interesting; Spiced watermelon salad; Lobster tails and Rack of Lamb. Great selection of special desserts. Vegetarian options.

MCGREGOR CAFE
4305 McGregor Blvd., Fort Myers, 239-936-1771
http://www.mcgregorcafe.com/
CUISINE: American
DRINKS: Full bar
SERVING: Breakfast, Lunch (closes at 3)
PRICE RANGE: $
Located in a former home in the historic McGregor section of downtown. (The *area* is historic, not this

old house, LOL.) Outdoor patio under a soaring canopy of oak trees is nice. Nothing fancy inside. What they offer is good solid American food (with some nods toward the Italian) and a friendly staff to go with it. Great **affordable** place for weekend brunch. Dogs welcome on the patio. All the usual breakfast items you'd expect, plus some good things for lunch: Beef & veal stuff tortellacci; Braised Pork Shank is bursting with flavor. They have a big selection of sandwiches and salads

OASIS RESTAURANT
2260 Dr Martin Luther King Blvd, Fort Myers, 239-334-1566
www.oasisatfortmyers.com
WEBSITE DOWN AT PRESSTIME
CUISINE: Pizza, Mediterranean
DRINKS: Beer & Wine Only
SERVING: B'fast & lunch, 6:30 to 3
PRICE RANGE: $
Serving locals for decades, this diner-style eatery offers a simple "tried & true" menu of American favorites. Very basic inside, not much different from an IHOP look, modern and utilitarian. Counter service as well as tables & booths. They have some outdoor seating, however, which is not like an IHOP. Menu picks: Great b'fast items, Grilled cheese & bacon and Turkey Rueben. Family-style eatery and the patio is pet-friendly.

OVER EASY CAFÉ
Olde Sanibel Shoppes, 630 Tarpon Bay Rd #1, Sanibel, 239-472-2625

CUISINE: Breakfast
DRINKS: Beer & Wine Only
SERVING: Breakfast & Lunch
PRICE RANGE: $$
Popular destination for breakfast and good reason as
they offer a creative menu including items like an
Egg Reuben sandwich and Smoked salmon benedict.
Also on the menu are homemade pancakes, omelets,
stuffed French toast, burgers and sandwiches.

PEACE RIVER SEAFOOD
5337 Duncan Rd, Punta Gorda, 941-505-8440
www.peaceriverseafood.com
CUISINE: Seafood
DRINKS: Beer & Wine Only
SERVING: Lunch & Dinner; closed Sun & Mon
PRICE RANGE: $$

This fish shack, a 1927 beat-up cracker cabin, is one of my favorite spots for seafood. It's about 20 minutes north of Fort Myers. It may get a little toasty in the summer, because it's all open air, but it's fun to sit there with newspapers on the table and listen to people banging crabs with their mallets. In the background you'll hear a parrot squawking out on the porch. Great choices like Steamed blue crab, shrimp and oysters. On-site market.

ROADHOUSE CAFÉ
15660 San Carlos Blvd, Fort Myers, 239-415-4375
www.roadhousecafefl.com
CUISINE: Steakhouse
DRINKS: Full Bar
SERVING: Dinner; closed Monday & Tuesday
PRICE RANGE: $$$
Upscale restaurant serving eclectic American fare. Favorites: Chicken Parmigiana and Cedar Planked Lemon Pepper Salmon, Live jazz nightly.

THE SANDBAR
2761 W Gulf Dr, Sanibel Island, 239-472-0305
www.sanibelsandbar.com
CUISINE: Steakhouse/Seafood
DRINKS: Full Bar
SERVING: Dinner; closed Sunday
PRICE RANGE: $$$
Upscale eatery serving steaks and seafood. Menu picks: Parmesan crusted grouper and Filet mignon. Vegetarian options available. Great wine selection.

THE SANIBEL SPROUT
Bailey's Center, 2463 Periwinkle Way, Sanibel, 239-472-4499
No Website
CUISINE: Juice Bar
DRINKS: No Booze
SERVING: Breakfast, Lunch & Dinner; closed Sun

PRICE RANGE: $$
Vegan café and juice bar with a varied menu
including items like Mexican salad and Emerald
mermaid smoothie. Great desserts. Vitamin
supplements sold here. Site of Sanibel/Captiiva
organic produce co-op every Wednesday.

SUNSET GRILL
6536 Pine Ave, Sanibel, 239-472-2333
www.sunsetgrillsanibel.com/
CUISINE: American/Seafood
DRINKS: Full Bar
SERVING: Breakfast, Lunch, Dinner
PRICE RANGE: $$
NEIGHBORHOOD: Fort Myers Beach
Lively beachfront eatery (it's across the highway
from the beach). Has a row of tables outside under
ceiling fans. From the inside, you look out large
windows to the water opposite. Dark wood floors,
friendly little place. Small bar with just a handful of
seats is very nice. The food's good, though not
terribly inspiring: crab cakes, seafood bisque,
bruschetta, a few salads, burgers, with entrees leaning
toward seafood (salmon, grouper, fish & chips), with
a pasta and a couple of steaks thrown in.

SWEET MELISSA'S CAFE
1625 Periwinkle Way, Sanibel, 239-472-1956
http://sweetmelissascafe.com/
CUISINE: American (New)
DRINKS: Full Bar
SERVING: Lunch & Dinner, Dinner only on
Saturdays: Closed on Sundays

PRICE RANGE: $$$
NEIGHBORHOOD: Sanibel Island
Upscale eatery with a bar that overlooks the kitchen.
Or you can opt for the main room with its white
tablecloths. They happily list their local supplies,
doing what they can to patronize these people, so they
get ingredients from Oakes Farm, Happy Foods, Blue
Star Seafood and others. Favorites: Fish Stew is
particularly good with a touch of saffron; Spice-
dusted grouper; Steamed mussels with frites; Tuna
timbale, featuring watermelon and avocado;
Blackened Redfish; smoked tenderloin (has a very
distinctive powerful flavor). Porch seating. Creative
cocktails and nice wine list. Top-notch desserts.

TIMBERS RESTAURANT & FISH MARKET
703 Tarpon Bay Rd, Sanibel Island, 239-395-2722
http://timbersofsanibel.com

CUISINE: Seafood
DRINKS: Full Bar
SERVING: Dinner
PRICE RANGE: $$
This popular eatery and combination fish market is known for its famous crunchy grouper. Great seafood specials. A locals' favorite year-round. The market is the go-to place to buy fish, steaks, and seafood. Gluten-free menu available. Nightly specials.

TRADERS CAFÉ
1551 Periwinkle Way, Sanibel, 239-472-7242
www.traderssanibel.com
CUISINE: Seafood
DRINKS: Full Bar
SERVING: Lunch & Dinner; closed Sun
PRICE RANGE: $$

This is a must-stop when visiting the island. A combination gift shop and eatery. Menu offers a great selection of seafood, steaks, and delicious desserts. Nice wine selection. Live entertainment on Tuesday and Thursday evenings. Nightly happy hour.

TRIAD SEAFOOD, EVERGLADES CITY
401 School Dr W, Everglades, 239-695-0722
www.triadseafoodmarketcafe.com
CUISINE: Seafood
DRINKS: Beer & Wine Only
SERVING: Lunch & Dinner; closes 6 p.m. during the week & 7 p.m. on weekends
PRICE RANGE: $$
A family owned and run eatery known for their "All You Can Eat" stone crabs. Patio dining. Reservations recommended.

VERANDA
2122 Second St., Fort Myers, 239-332-2065
www.verandarestaurant.com
CUISINE: Southern Regional
DRINKS: Full bar
SERVING: Lunch & Dinner
PRICE RANGE: $$
Housed in two 100-year-old homes, with outdoor dining in the garden courtyard. Romantic setting, extensive wine list and first class service.

WHERE TO SHOP

BASS PRO SHOP
Gulf Town Center
10040 Gulf Center Dr., Fort Myers, 239-461-7800
www.basspro.com/
For any kind of outdoor sporting gear, this is the
place. Hunting, fishing, boating, shooting, camping,
shoes, boots, clothing (men's, women's, kids').
Absolutely super place to find a creative gift.

ESTERRA SPA & SALON
6231 Estero Blvd., Fort Myers Beach, 239-765-4772
www.esterraspa.com
Spa with 4 locations in SW Florida. Services
available include Swedish Massage, European Facial,
Body Scrubs, Pedicures, and hair cuts.

FAMILY THRIFT CENTER
4231 Colonial Blvd., Fort Myers, 239-274-8821
www.familythrift.com/
Store Hours: M - S: 9-6; Sun: 12-5
In the building formerly housing 84 Lumber, you'll
find a great selection of clothing for the whole family.
New items and designer labels: White House / Black
Market, Lucky, Gap, Aeropostale, Tommy Hilfiger,
The Limited, Children's Place. Accessory department
has finds from Coach, Louis Vuitton, Gucci, Guess,
Vera Bradley and others. A vast array of books for all
ages. Educational toys, dolls, stuffed animals and
many other fun things for children, all priced to sell.
Household items, Furniture, Electronics, Jewelry,
Music.

FLEAMASTERS FLEAMARKET
4135 MLK Blvd., Fort Myers, 239-334-7001
www.fleamall.com/
From Cleveland Avenue, go east on Dr. M.L. King Jr.
Blvd. (SR 82) for 3.2 miles, look for Fleamasters on
the left.
This place is nothing if not festive. Get everything
from a pair of shoes to a week's worth of fresh
produce from one of their hundreds of bargain packed
booths. You'll find outlets for many name brands,
fashions, resort wear and home decor. Plus an eclectic
mix of arts and crafts, antiques and collectibles, food
treats. Want a shell wind chime? Get it here. Shell
shops sell sea fans, shell night-lights, shell jewelry,
even alligator heads. Golf shops, fishing tackle
outlets, and sportswear stores, tool stores.

OLD TIME POTTERY
4450 Fowler St., Fort Myers, 239-278-1141
www.oldtimepottery.com/
9 to 9 except on Sunday, when it's 9 to 7.
Great selection of goods here, a huge selection of
baskets, bakeware, floral, cookware, cutlery,
dinnerware, flatware, gadgets, glassware, linens, rugs,
pillows.

THE SWAP SHOP
17851 Pine Ridge Rd., Fort Myers Beach, 239-432-
0906
No web site.
Lots of little finds.

SHIPWRECK TREASURES
237 Old San Carlos Blvd, Fort Myers Beach, 239-
765-1561
www.motelfortmyersbeach.com
A mix of touristy stuff and the occasional off-beat
item. Fun to browse.

TUTTLES SEAHORSE SHELL SHOP
362 Periwinkle Way Sanibel Island, 239-472-0707
www.tuttlesseahorse.com
Open since 1973, this shop offers an eclectic selection
of tropical treasures and trinkets including sterling
silver, bracelets, earrings, and toe rings.

VANPELT JEWELERS
12377 S Cleveland Ave., Ste 14, Fort Myers, 239-
275-7300
No web site
Nice general selection at fair prices.

WHAT TO
SEE & DO

BABCOCK WILDERNESS ADVENTURES
8000 State Road 31, Punta Gorda, 800-500-5583
www.babcockwilderness.com
ADMISSION: fees vary
A 90-minute Eco-Tour that shows you the sights and
sounds of the Babcock Ranch which encompasses a
90,000-acre area. Visitors will see a working ranch
with cowhands on quarter horses working the cattle
herds. Also available are recreational hunting
opportunities, annual hunting leases, horseback

riding, and hiking in the preserve. There used to be quite a few of these huge cattle ranches, but this is the last one.

BILLY'S RENTAL BIKES
1470 Periwinkle Way, Sanibel, 239-472-5248
www.billysrentals.coms
Rentals include bikes – children's and adults, Segways, beach wheelchairs, beach umbrellas, sand chairs, scooters, and two or four passenger surreys. Delivery available for multiple day rentals.

CLINIC FOR REHABILITATION OF WILDLIFE (CROW)
3883 Sanibel Captiva Rd, Sanibel, 239-472-3644
www.crowclinic.org
This organization cares for over 3,500 wildlife patients yearly including more than 200 species of sick, injured and orphaned wildlife creatures. The organization also runs an educational fellowship and externship program for students.

BILLY'S RENTAL BIKES
1470 Periwinkle Way, Sanibel, 239-472-5248
www.billysrentals.coms
Rentals include bikes – children's and adults, Segways, beach wheelchairs, beach umbrellas, sand chairs, scooters, and two or four passenger surreys. Delivery available for multiple day rentals.

CLINIC FOR REHABILITATION OF WILDLIFE (CROW)
3883 Sanibel Captiva Rd, Sanibel, 239-472-3644

www.crowclinic.org

This organization cares for over 3,500 wildlife patients yearly including more than 200 species of sick, injured and orphaned wildlife creatures. The organization also runs an educational fellowship and externship program for students.

BAILEY-MATTHEWS SHELL MUSEUM

3075 Sanibel Captiva Rd, Sanibel, 239-395-2233

http://www.shellmuseum.org/

CLOSED TEMPORARILY FOR RENOVATIONS

HOURS: Open daily

ADMISSION: Moderate fee

Museum focusing on seashells, conchology, malacology, and the study of shells. Operates as an information and reference center for scientists, students, and shell enthusiasts. Museum features 34 exhibitions of shells from all over the world.

DOG BEACH

8800 Estero Blvd., Fort Myers Beach, 239-707-1874

www.leeparks.org/

If you have a dog, bring it here. (Low tide is preferable.) You'll find this located just off Estero Boulevard, north of Bonita Beach and south of Lover's Key State Park.

EDISON & FORD WINTER ESTATES

2350 McGregor Blvd., Fort Myers, 239-334-7419
www.edisonfordwinterestates.org/
TOURS: open from 9 to 5:30, with the last guided
tour setting off at 4.

It's just as well these two estates share a common
name now their owners are dead, because Thomas
Edison and Henry Ford were such great friends in
life. It all started in 1885, when Edison came to what
was no more than a tiny settlement on the
Caloosahatchee River. Here he bought 14 acres and
started building his house and factory where he
continued his work inventing things. (His principal
residence was in West Orange, N.J.).

Friends like Henry Ford and Harvey Firestone
visited him and bought parcels nearby so they could
enjoy the beautiful Florida winter climate Edison had
embraced. Ford bought his house in 1916, and you'll
get to see the splendid view of the Caloosahatchee
River that Ford enjoyed from the "Ford Porch."

The complex joins the Ford house next door, and now includes about 20 acres of historical buildings, very special gardens (Edison collected plant specimens and people sent them to him from all over the world—he planted them here in botanical gardens that remain to this day).

Here you'll see the Edison Main House, the Guest House he built for long-term visitors, the Edison Botanic Research Lab and the Edison Ford Museum, which offers an impressive array of inventions, artifacts and special exhibit galleries.

Fascinating is the banyan tree you encounter right after the parking lot. It looks on first glance to be a hammock or a small forest of trees, but really all the trunks are aerial roots of the same tree, a tree Edison himself planted in 1925. A sign tells you that it was sent to Edison by Firestone, who knew that one of Edison's goals was to generate a source for rubber here in the U.S. so America wouldn't have to rely on foreign sources in the event of a war that could cut off our supply. (Remember, Firestone made tires!)

You'll be interested to see that when Thomas Edison took a "vacation," it most certainly was a working vacation. His lab had room not only for himself, but a group of scientists he brought down to work with him. He never stopped.

There's an exhibit detailing Edison's camping trips into the Everglades with Ford. Ford even supplied a motorized "chuck wagon," adapting one of his cars into perhaps the first RV which was loaded with food and supplies to accompany them on their adventures into the wild.

FLORIDA REPERTORY THEATER
2267 Bay St., Fort Myers, 239-332-4488
www.floridarep.org
ADMISSION: Ticket prices vary per performance.
BOX OFFICE HOURS: Mon. - Fri. 10am-5pm and 1 hour before curtain times during season.
Florida Repertory Theater is a professional theater company offering full scale productions in The Arcade Theater, built in 1908. Check out the website for current production schedule.

GOOD TIME CHARTERS
4765 Estero Blvd., Fort Myers Beach, 239-218-8014
www.goodtimecharter.com/
Paddleboarding, shelling, kayak tours, dolphin tours, wildlife, fishing charters.

HOLIDAY WATER SPORTS
Pink Shell Beach Resort & Spa
200 Estero Blvd., 239-765-4386
Best Western Beach Resort
684 Estero Blvd., 239-463-6778
DiamondHead Beach Resort
2000 Estero Blvd., 239-765-2252
www.holidaywatersportsfmb.com/
Has 3 locations on Fort Myers Beach. Wave runners,
parasailing, dolphin tours, boat rentals, water craft,
beach services, fishing charters, pretty much anything
having to do with water sports, these people can set
you up.

IMAG
2000 Cranford Ave, Fort Myers, 239-321-7420
https://theimag.org
HOURS: Open daily
ADMISSION: Minimal fee

A hands-on science and aquarium museum that offers a yearly summer camp. The museum features a popular dinosaur dig and many interactive exhibitions. Families can enjoy the hands-on aquarium and 3-D movie. Suggestion: pack a lunch as there is only a hot dog cart on premises.

J. C. CRUISES
2313 Edwards Dr., Fort Myers, 239-334-7474
www.jccruises.com
J.C. Cruises offers a variety of tours on the scenic Caloosahatchee River on a 600-passenger paddlewheel boat. Some cruises offer a four-hour buffet, dancing, sunbathing. There are also sightseeing cruises on an 80-passenger boat. Reservations required. Boats sail from the Fort Myers Yacht Basin in downtown.

J.N. "DING" DARLING NATIONAL WILDLIFE REFUGE
1 Wildlife Dr, Sanibel, 239-472-1100

http://dingdarlingsociety.org/
HOURS: Open daily
ADMISSION: Free
Named for the cartoonist Jay Norwood "Ding" Darling, this refuge is part of the United States National Wildlife Refuge System and is known for its abundant bird life. The refuge sponsors summer camp and free summer activities. Bookstore on site. Wildlife trail for biking and exploring (closed on Fridays). On-site fishing (minimal fee).

JUNGLE GOLF
17710 San Carlos Blvd., Fort Myers Beach, 239-466-9797
www.junglegolfminigolf.com/
9am to 11pm (verify hours off season)
This is the best putt-putt in the area. Thought it's been here for about 20 years, it is meticulously maintained.

Another plus: it actually has "terrain," with hills and valleys, giving even the adults some tougher than usual shots to work out.

LEE COUNTY MANATEE PARK
10901 State Road 80 (Palm Beach Blvd.), Fort Myers, 239-6690-5030
www.leeparks.org
ADMISSION: Free. There are fees for parking.
HOURS: 8 a.m. to 5 p.m. through March, then until 8 p.m.
Park offers opportunity to observe manatees in their natural habitat. During the winter, as many as 100 manatees, some with calves, are visible from an overlook. Also available: free guided walks, shelter rentals, manatee activity workbook and facts.

OFF SHORE SAILING SCHOOL
Pink Shell Beach Resort & Marina, 275 Estero Blvd, Fort Myers Beach, 239-463-8650
www.offshoresailing.com
Great destination for a sailing vacation with incredible beachfront views and 1500 feet of white sand stretching along the Gulf of Mexico. Classes teach sailing at all levels.

PARADISE PARASAIL
1160 Estero Blvd., Fort Myers Beach, 239-463-7272
www.paradiseparasail.com/
Paradise Parasail's chutes are flown by USCG-licensed captains. After harnessing up to 6 people into the smiley face chute, the wind naturally hoists riders aloft while the 600-1,200 foot line sails the riders up to 500 feet above the water. From this height, the riders can enjoy the breathtaking views of Fort Myers Beach or Lake of the Ozarks. Once capturing the astonishing views, riders have the option to do "free fall dips." You can have a relaxing dip that just allows your toes to touch the water or a real free fall that gets you soaked. Professional photographers on board will give you 40 to 60 pictures and a short action video.

SALTY SAM'S PIRATE CRUISE
Salty Sam's Marina
2500 Main St., Fort Myers Beach, 239-765-7272
www.floridapiratecruise.com/

This is a 90-minute "pirate cruise" aboard a replica of a Spanish galleon. The kids will love it.

SANIBEL-CAPTIVA CONSERVATION FOUNDATION
3333 Sanibel Captiva Rd, Sanibel, 239-472-2329
www.sccf.org/
This foundation is dedicated to conservation of coastal habitats and aquatic resources on Sanibel and Captiva. The foundation conducts research in many areas including sea grasses, mangroves, fish population, and shellfish restoration. Educational programs are offered. Activities include beach walks, trail walks, boat tours, wading trips, kayak tours, and classroom-based activities. The Nature Center boasts four miles of trails, an observation tower, exhibits, a touch tank, butterfly house, and a Nature Shop.

SANIBEL ISLAND
www.sanibelisland.com
A popular family-friendly vacation spot where you can find lots to keep the kids occupied. Lots of white sand, beach activities, shopping, golf, restaurants, and family accommodations. Many hotels offer kid's programs. The island boasts lush tropical foliage and crystal blue water. It's only a 3-mile causeway ride away from the comparatively busy Fort Myers.

Some 70% of the island is preserved as wildlife refuge, which is good for us and good for the wildlife. Here you won't see stoplights, billboards, or even street lamps. No high-rise buildings either.

The Calusa Indians lived here for some 5,000 years until invading Europeans wiped them out. (I wonder what the Calusa policy was toward illegal immigrants. LOL.)

These Indians used the plentiful shells that washed up on the pristine beaches (that much hasn't changed—the beaches are prehistorically perfect) for everything from weapons to money to bodily decorations like necklaces. Because Sanibel and its western neighbor Captiva are situated east-west rather than north-south, they catch shells churned up by the Gulf currents.

One of the world's largest mangrove stands is here, and you can see for yourself the manatees, alligators, conchs and other creatures that come here for shelter.

The locals are quick to point out the difference between a "refuse" and a "park." Parks are for people, they'll tell you, and refuges are for animals.

President Truman established this refuge in 1945, convinced by political cartoonist J.N. "Ding" Darling.

SEA TREK DEEP SEA FISHING
702 Fisherman's Wharf, Fort Myers Beach, 239-765-7665
www.seatrekfishing.com/
The 65-foot SeaTrek offers Deep Sea Fishing for half-day, full-day or several day trips. Doesn't matter if you're experienced or not. It's fun even if you just want to spend the day in the sun. They also have private charters, special deep water trips, and Dry Tortugas trips throughout the year or can arrange cruises for weddings or other special events.

SOUTHWEST FLORIDA MUSEUM OF HISTORY

2031 Jackson St., Fort Myers, 239-321-7430
www.museumofhistory.org
ADMISSION: fees vary
Admission includes audio tour. Museum members are always free.
HOURS: Tuesday through Saturday 10 a.m. – 5 p.m. Closed Sundays and Mondays.
The history of Southwest Florida explored from prehistoric era through the ages. Permanent collection is housed in the former Atlantic Coastline Railroad depot. Recent exhibitions include exhibit titled "Land of Giants: Paleo Florida." "The museum also hosts a variety of touring exhibitions.

SUN HARVEST CITRUS

14601 6-Mile Cypress Pkwy, Fort Myers, 239-768-2686

www.sunharvestcitrus.com/

The Sun Harvest Citrus retail store and packinghouse offer a variety of citrus based products including honey, key lime pies, marmalades & jellies, candies, fresh juices, pecans, salad dressings, gift sets and a selection of Florida fruit wines (which are pretty God-awful unless you drink them so cold you can't taste them).

INDEX

71